COMPETITIVE
FIGURE SKATING
FOR GIRLS

KATHRYN M. MONCRIEF

the rosen publishing group's
rosen
central

Published in 2001 by The Rosen Publishing Group, Inc.
29 East 21st Street, New York, NY 10010

First Edition

Library of Congress Cataloging-in-Publication Data

Moncrief, Kathryn M.
Competitive figure skating for girls/by Kathryn M. Moncrief.—1st ed.
p. cm. — (Sportsgirl)
Includes bibliographical references and index.
ISBN 0-8239-3403-9 (lib. bdg.)
1. Skating—Juvenile literature. 2. Women skaters—Juvenile literature. [1. Ice skating. 2. Women skaters.] I. Title. II. Series.
GV850.4 .M64 2001
796.91'2'082—dc21
                                        2001000917

Manufactured in the United States of America

Contents

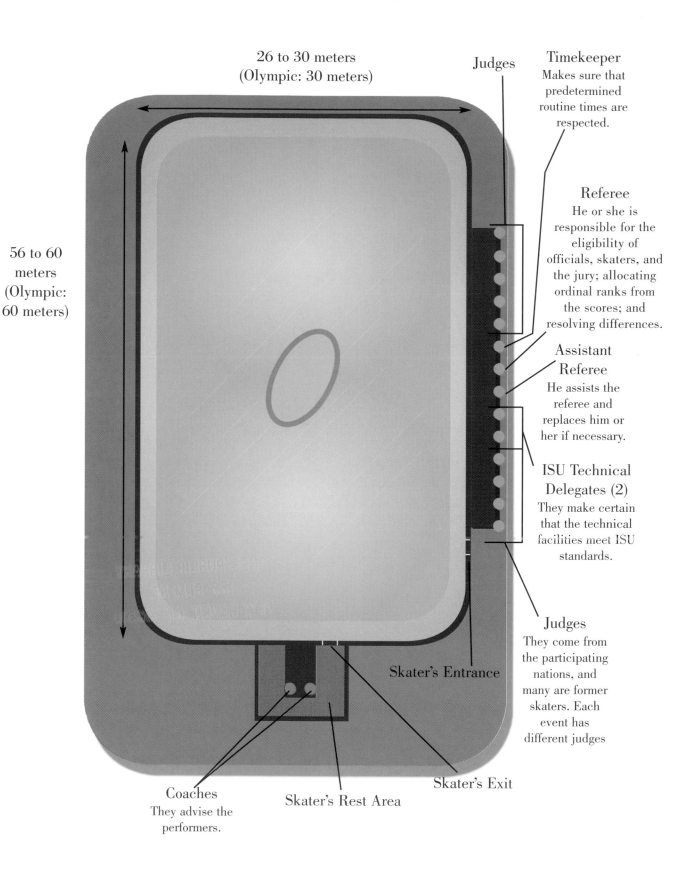

26 to 30 meters
(Olympic: 30 meters)

Judges

Timekeeper
Makes sure that predetermined routine times are respected.

Referee
He or she is responsible for the eligibility of officials, skaters, and the jury; allocating ordinal ranks from the scores; and resolving differences.

Assistant Referee
He assists the referee and replaces him or her if necessary.

ISU Technical Delegates (2)
They make certain that the technical facilities meet ISU standards.

56 to 60 meters
(Olympic: 60 meters)

Skater's Entrance

Judges
They come from the participating nations, and many are former skaters. Each event has different judges

Coaches
They advise the performers.

Skater's Rest Area

Skater's Exit

Introduction

Speed, balance, flexibility, athleticism, lyricism, power. Nothing feels better than skimming the ice on one-eighth of an inch of steel, breathing the crisp, cold air, and hearing the sound of blades on ice. Nothing is more exhilarating than learning a new spin or landing a big jump at just the right time. Figure skating combines athletic skill and artistic expression in a unique and beautiful sport.

Today, skating is a multimillion-dollar activity with competitions, shows, and tours; it is second only to NFL football in the size of audience it draws, and skating champions such as Michelle Kwan and Tara Lipinski are well-known celebrities. But figure skating is also a sport that can be enjoyed by girls and women of all ages and sizes, from two years old up to women in their seventies. Whether you skate competitively or recreationally, the sport builds self-esteem and confidence, gives you a sense of accomplishment and a toned, healthy body, and lets you have fun.

Ginger Clayton and Patty Hall perform in the Ice Follies of 1954. In recent years, figure skating has evolved into a multimillion-dollar industry.

Why is the sport called figure skating? The name comes from the "figures" carved in the ice by the skate blades. School, or compulsory, figures range from simple to complex designs, including figure eights, loops, and brackets. Each figure must be traced, then skated over in exactly the same way two more times. At one time, there were more than eighty figures that could be skated in competition. Judges considered both the excellence of the tracing on the ice and the posture of the skater while he or she executed the figure.

In 1990, figures were abolished from competition, though the name "figure skating" remains. Now that they don't have to spend so much time and money practicing figures, many young skaters are able to rise to top levels much more quickly than in the past. Some skaters, however, miss the figures for the level of focus and discipline and the special skills, especially the emphasis on edges and control, that figures brought to the sport.

Ice-skating has a long history. It began in what is now northern Europe thousands of years ago. First bone runners, then metal runners, were strapped to shoes.

The first skating club was formed in Edinburgh, Scotland, in 1742. But it wasn't until 1850 that figure skates with the blades permanently attached to boots were invented, and figure skating in both Europe and North America really took off. Skating clubs began holding competitions and ice carnivals. The oldest skating club in the United States, the Philadelphia Skating Club and Humane Society, was incorporated in 1861.

But figure skating was still stiff and formal. Then, in the 1860s, an American skater, Jackson Haines, revolutionized skating by incorporating dance moves and skating to music in his routines. His signature moves included a sit-spin and a spiral. He skated on tour, and his style quickly caught on.

In 1892, what is now the International Skating Union (ISU) was formed to govern speed- and ice-skating. Now, the ISU has more than fifty member countries. There are competitive skaters from countries as diverse as the United States, Canada, China, Russia, Uzbekistan, and Thailand.

At first, competitive figure skating was considered a man's sport. People believed it was unsuitable for a woman to pursue such an athletic activity or to show her legs when her skirt came up a bit during jumps. In 1902, Madge Syers of Great Britain shocked the skating world by entering and coming in second in the men's world championships. In 1903, women were officially barred! But women weren't about to give up. In 1906, a separate ladies' event was introduced. Madge Syers went on to win the ladies' world gold medal in both 1906 and 1907, as well as the 1908 Olympic gold medal, when skating first appeared at the summer games. In 1924, when the separate winter Olympics was first started, skating became, as it is today, a part of the winter games.

In the 1920s and 1930s, another famous skater, Sonja Henie of Norway, captured the public's imagination and had a major impact on the popularity of the sport. She was only eleven years old when she competed in her first Olympics in 1924. She came in eighth. However, by 1927, at age fourteen, she was the world champion. Altogether, she won ten world titles and three Olympic gold medals. After she retired from amateur competition, she toured in popular ice shows and even became a film star. Henie was especially known for her dazzling skating skills, which combined ballet with skating, and for her innovative, glamorous costumes. Before Henie, women skated in long skirts for the sake of modesty! Henie, skating in short dresses, which were acceptable only because she was so young, was able to do spins and jumps that had been impossible in long, heavy dresses. Also, Henie was the first to wear the white figure skating boots that are most common for women today.

Sonja Henie not only brought women's figure skating to a higher level of competition, but she also had a successful film career, starring in many movies.

The Basics

You are interested in skating. Now you need ice! There are ice rinks located in almost every town and city. Check your local mall, school, recreation center, or specialized skating facility for ice times. You will find "public sessions," which are times that allow all skaters on the ice. Public sessions are inexpensive, but they can be a nuisance for anyone who is there to practice figure skating skills. The rink can be crowded with skaters of all ability levels. Skating is limited to one direction with only the center reserved for figure skating practice.

Instead, you may want to look for "freestyle sessions," which give freestyle skaters a chance to practice. These are often divided into "high" and "low" levels of ability. Although they're more expensive than public sessions, they have the advantage of ice reserved expressly for figure skaters. Other sessions may be reserved especially for ice dancing. Some rinks host special events like "adults only" time or "family night." Find a session that suits your ability level and skating preference.

Finally, the rink may offer "club ice," available only to members of the local figure skating club. Consider becoming a member of the club. There will be a fee to join, but benefits include reserved ice sessions, socializing, and other member privileges.

What You Will Need

You won't need to make a big investment to get started, but at the very minimum you will need a pair of skates and some workout clothes.

Skates

Skates consist of boots and blades. Try rental skates before you invest in your own pair, when you're sure you want to continue. If you do continue to skate, you will soon want to have your own skates. To keep costs down, look for a used, but not broken down, pair of boots to begin. Do not buy boots with deep crevices and signs of excessive wear. Try your local pro shop, or check bulletin boards at your rink for leads on good-quality used skates.

Whether you are skating in rental skates or your own pair, find skates that fit and feel good on your feet. Properly fitted boots and blades will increase your comfort and will help your skating. Boots should be snug but not tight, and your foot should not move in the heel. Instead of heavy socks or double layers of socks, wear tights or light stockings. Lace your skates so they are snug at the toes but a little looser around your ankles so they can move when you bend your knees. Ask a coach or a professional at your local pro shop to help you find the best fit. Look for leather soles, not molded plastic ones, and steel blades that can be sharpened. Avoid inexpensive hardware or discount store skates. Reputable brands include Don Jackson, Graff, Harlick, Reidell, and SP-Teri.

Be careful not to purchase "too much boot." Boots that are too advanced, or too thick and heavy, for your skating level will be more difficult for you to break in and will hinder your progress. Boots need the right amount of padding and stiffness to support you when you skate. As you progress (as you jump more), you will need thicker boots to withstand the additional pressure.

Boots can be very uncomfortable at first and can take time to break in. Be patient about finding the right pair and getting a good fit. The boots, along with your blades, are your most important pieces of equipment. As you advance as a skater, you may eventually want to consider custom boots made just for you. These are more expensive, but they'll be precisely constructed both for your feet and for the type of training you do.

As a beginner, you can purchase stock (premade) boots with blades already mounted. A beginning boot and blade combination costs approximately $100 to $200. When you purchase higher-quality skates, boots and blades will be sold separately. As with choosing your boots, you must select blades that are appropriate for your size, ability, and the type of skating you do.

As a figure skater, your skates are your most important pieces of equipment. It is essential that you care for and maintain them properly.

Wearing proper warm-up and workout gear is essential, as the ice rink can be very cold.

For example, ice-dance blades are shorter and have smaller toe picks than do freestyle blades. This is because ice dancers do not execute jumps like freestyle skaters, who need large picks to help them vault into the air. Blades differ in radius (how curved they are), hollowness (the groove between the edges), and toe pick. Again, work with your coach or a pro in selecting blades. Blades will cost from $200 to $600. Remember to have a professional mount your blades to your boots, as correct placement is crucial.

How long your skates will last depends on how often you train (especially how much you jump) and how much you grow. If you

Anyone can skate at Rockefeller Center, one of the most famous
ice-skating rinks in the world.

train on an elite level, your skates will last for about six months
to a year, and your blades for about nine months. If you are a
recreational skater, they will last much longer. You can use your
boots until they are broken down (until they no longer provide
you with proper support) and your blades until they can no
longer be sharpened.

Blades should always be kept sharp and in good condition.
New blades need to be sharpened before you first use them.
After that, they'll need sharpening about once a month,
depending on how much skating you do. Have a professional
sharpen your blades.

Skate Guards

Skate guards, which are rubber covers for your blades, protect them from nicks, pebbles, and dirt on the floor after you put on your boots. Never walk with your skates on without your guards, even for short distances. Remember to remove the guards before you step out onto the ice. Everyone has made that mistake at least once. The hard fall that results is usually enough to remind you to take the guards off the next time! You will also need a pair of soakers (terry cloth blade covers) to protect your blades from moisture.

After you skate, be sure to wipe your blades dry with a towel to prevent rust and to cover the blades with your soakers. Remember not to store your skates in a closed bag when you get home. Remove them so they can air out and dry. Periodically, you will want to polish your boots (especially before a test or a competition!) to keep them looking fresh.

Novice skaters may find it helpful, and cheaper, to train in group lessons.

Practice Clothing

Clothing for practice should be warm and comfortable, and it should allow you to move. Street clothes, such as jeans, will not give you the necessary flexibility, but you don't need special costumes or expensive dance clothes for practice either. Workout clothes, a simple skating dress, a leotard and tights, or leggings and a T-shirt are perfectly acceptable. Cover up with a sweater, sweatshirt, or warm-up jacket and sweatpants or leg warmers you can take off when you get hot. You should have a pair of light, stretchy gloves to keep your hands warm and to protect them when you fall. You might also want a pair of boot covers if you find that your toes get too cold. Finally, if you have long hair, you will want to wear it in a ponytail or braid to keep your hair out of your face.

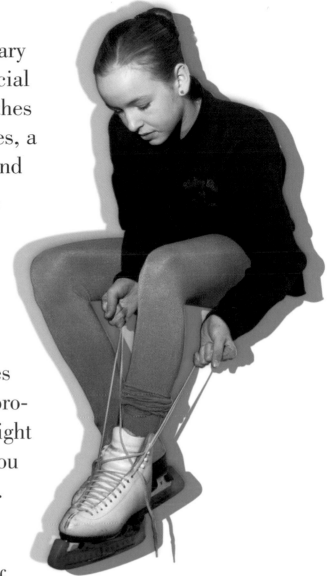

Skate guards protect your blades from dirt and other materials on the floor.

Protective Gear

Many beginners use pads and helmets to help prevent injury. A good bicycle helmet will do. You may also want wrist guards like those used for in-line skating, as well as soft elbow and knee pads. These items are easily available at a sporting goods store.

Skating can be fun for the whole family.

Miscellaneous

There are a few more things you will want to have in your skate bag. Bring tissues. Noses tend to run in the cold air. It is helpful to have foam pads (you can use makeup sponges) or, even better, gel pads (sold under the brand name Bunga Pads) to slip into your skates when you need to help protect your feet from rubbing. Bring bandages for blisters that may develop from your skates. Always have an extra pair of laces on hand in case you break one. Other useful things include extra tights and socks, extra gloves, and lip balm.

2 Elements

It takes many years of training to skate at a high level because skating skills are complex and cumulative. For example, you need to learn a bunny hop in order to learn a waltz jump. You need to be able to do a waltz jump, as well as all of your other single-rotation jumps, before you can learn an axel jump. And you need to master all of your single jumps before you can move onto doubles, then triples.

It's like learning to play a musical instrument: You must first learn the basic skills, then practice them until they are part of you. Some jumps and spins take years to perfect. But you can gain a sense of accomplishment as you learn and become proficient at each new skill on the way to achieving your goals in the sport. Talent and natural physical ability certainly help, but 80 percent of the sport is mental. Skating requires desire, focus, dedication, and practice time. Most of all, it should be something you enjoy doing. You don't have to begin skating at age three or be a size three to skate either. Skating is a sport that anyone can enjoy.

Learning the Basics

The best way to get started is to join a "learn to skate" program at your local rink. The Ice Skating Institute (ISI), the United States Figure Skating Association (USFSA), and Skate Canada all have "learn to skate" programs. All three administer tests and host competitions, and all three have very good, structured programs for learning basic skating skills. The ISI focuses its attention primarily on the recreational skater. The USFSA and Skate Canada, as the national governing bodies for skating in the United States and Canada, are more oriented toward the competitive (Olympic-eligible) skater. Being a member of one of these organizations also makes you eligible to participate in their testing and competition system.

A series of group lessons will cover basic skills, including proper stroking, gliding, falling, and stopping. It will then progress to turns, beginning spins, and jumps. You can learn all of your basic skills and beginning freestyle moves in a group lesson program. Group lessons will cost about $80 for eight one-hour, weekly lessons. Each session will include both instruction and practice time.

If you hire a private coach, you can learn more skills in a shorter period of time, and you will receive greater one-on-one attention.

Jump Identification (Beginning with the Least Difficult)

Waltz jump A basic half jump, the foundation of the axel. It begins going forward on a left outside edge and lands on the right outside edge of the opposite foot.

Toe loop A toe jump that takes off from a back outside edge, assisted by pushing up and off the opposite toe pick, and lands on the same back outside edge. The same jump is a toe walley when taking off from the inside edge.

Salchow An edge jump that takes off from the back inside edge and lands on the back outside edge of the opposite foot. It was invented by Ulrich Salchow of Sweden.

Loop jump   An edge jump that takes off and lands from the back outside edge of the same foot. This jump is sometimes called a Rittberger after Germany's Werner Rittberger, who invented it.

Flip jump   A toe jump that takes off from the back inside edge, assisted by the toe pick, and lands on the back outside edge of the opposite foot.

Lutz jump   A toe jump invented by Austrian skater Alois Lutz that takes off from a long, back outside edge, assisted by the toe pick, and lands on the back outside edge of the opposite foot. An intended lutz that switches to an inside edge is often referred to as a "flutz."

Axel jump   An edge jump that takes off from a forward outside edge and lands on the back outside edge of the opposite foot. This is considered the most difficult jump because it rotates an extra half turn in the air. For example, a triple axel rotates three and one half times. It was invented by Norway's Axel Paulsen.

On the left, the skater demonstrates the snowplow; on the right, she performs a two-foot turn.

at the arch of the right foot. (Your feet will form the T.) Push off with the right foot and allow yourself to glide forward on the left. Keep your free leg off the ice and extended behind you with your leg turned out as you push, then bring it back to you and shift your weight onto it. Push off with the opposite leg. Repeat and continue.

Snowplow Stop

Once you learn to go forward, you will need to know how to stop. The snowplow stop is the easiest way to stop your forward momentum. Point the toes of your skate together to make an upside-down V shape, like the front a snowplow. Press down and out with the inside of both blades, remembering to keep your knees bent, until you come to a stop. Skate blades move smoothly across the ice only in a forward or backward motion. Here, you are scraping the blade in a sideways motion, which will bring you to a stop. You can also do this stop by turning in just one foot, instead of both feet. In this case, continue gliding on one foot, but turn in the toe of the other blade. Press down and out until you come to a stop.

Two-Foot Turn

Gliding forward on two feet, rotate your upper body in a clockwise or counterclockwise direction. Let your hip follow, letting your body work like a spring as you turn from going forward to backward.

Nutrition

In skating, eating disorders can sometimes be a problem. As a performance sport, competitive figure skating focuses attention on body weight and size. Some girls feel that they must conform to a particular ideal to be a skater. However, drastic and unhealthy measures—such as fasting—will drain you of the energy you need to succeed on the ice. If you find yourself worrying about your weight or size, please consult with a physician to evaluate the situation. You don't need to be twig-thin to participate in and enjoy skating! In fact, you need a balanced, healthy diet if you're going to have enough stamina and energy.

You must master the basics before you can begin learning artistic moves, such as the spin seen here.

Off-Ice Training

In addition to lessons and practice at the rink, you can also participate in other activities to enhance your skating. These include weight training and dance classes, including jazz, modern, ballet, or others. Consult with your coach to determine which activities are best for you.

3

Tests and Competition

Training, testing, and competition go together. Competitions on the regional, national, and international level work toward membership on an Olympic or world team or winning a medal at one of those competitions. Training and competing are about more than just winning a medal, though. You can test and compete to challenge yourself, to judge your progress, and to have a goal to motivate you in your training. However, you can enjoy skating without ever testing or competing. The choice to compete or not to compete is a personal one.

Tests

Once you learn to skate, you should take tests administered by the USFSA, the ISI, or Skate Canada. You can test just for the personal satisfaction of

Judges examine a skater as she traces her compulsory figures on the ice at the 1990 World Figure Skating Championships. This was the last time a competition required compulsory figures.

knowing what you have accomplished. But if you choose to compete, you will need to test to determine your level of competition. The skaters you see on television are, with only a few exceptions, senior or championship-level skaters. However, there are many competitive levels below the senior level and most skaters are in the lower levels, working their way up. The USFSA levels, beginning at the bottom, are pre-preliminary, preliminary, pre-juvenile, juvenile, intermediate, novice, junior, and senior.

In the ISI system, staff members administer tests. You can earn badges when you compete at each level. ISI levels, from the lowest to the highest, are pre-alpha, alpha, beta, gamma, and delta. Once you have passed the delta test, you can begin working on freestyle levels, beginning at freestyle 1. You can test at each level anytime you and your coach decide you are ready. Information on ISI testing is available by contacting the ISI (see the For More Information section at the end of this book).

The USFSA is more regimented because it is oriented toward competitive skaters. Coaches administer tests only at the lowest levels. Test sessions must by sanctioned by the USFSA board of directors and are judged by qualified officials. The panel of judges (usually three) watches your performance and gives you a "pass" or a "retry," meaning you will have to take the test again in the future to advance. The judges may also supply comments for your improvement. Contact the USFSA for information on testing requirements and procedures.

Competition

Whatever your skating goals, there are many types of competitions at every ability level, from local and club events to national and international events. Whether you plan to compete in the nationals or an interclub competition, competitions can be both motivating and fun.

ISI Competitions

The ISI, focusing on the recreational skater, offers many different competitions, including events for solo dancers, small children, skaters with disabilities, comedy teams, production numbers, interpretive skaters, and so on.

Most of the figure skaters you see on television are senior or championship-level skaters.

USFSA Competitions

The USFSA, geared more toward Olympic-eligible competitors, offers both invitational events (stand-alone competitions hosted by skating clubs) and qualifying events (those that determine eligibility for higher-level competitions and national or Olympic teams). The rules for USFSA competitions are specified by the International Skating Union (ISU), which is the governing body for figure skating. An ISU committee meets regularly to review and to revise rules. Be certain that you and your coach are aware of the most recent rule changes when you are preparing for competition.

A system of qualifying events on the regional, sectional, and national levels begins in the fall and culminates in the junior nationals for juvenile and intermediate skaters, and the senior nationals for novice, junior, and senior skaters. Regional and sectional competitions determine who will qualify for nationals. Only four skaters from each section—Pacific coast, midwestern and eastern—advance to nationals. Other skaters, including champions from the previous year,

Judges score skating competitions on a scale of 0 to 6. Each score is two marks, one ranking a skater's technique, and the other rating her performance.

are also allowed to compete. The national championships determine who will represent the country on world and Olympic teams, though a selection committee has the final say. Also in the fall, junior and senior international competitions leading to a grand prix final take place, as do European and the Four Continents championships.

The final and most prestigious event in non-Olympic years is the world championship. The number of competitors that each country is allowed is determined by that country's placing in the previous year's world championship, but each country may send only three skaters at most.

Scoring

A skating competition is scored by a panel of judges. The skater with the highest marks wins. A referee monitors the action and is the person who decides what should be done if a skater has a problem—like a costume coming undone, or music skipping during the program. The referee decides if and when the skater may begin again.

Scoring is on a scale of 0 (not skated) to 6 (perfect, no deductions). The best score a skater can receive is a perfect 6.0. Each score is made up of two marks: the first for technical merit (the skater's technique) and the second for presentation (the skater's performance).

Length of a Performance

The junior- or senior-level short program lasts for two minutes and forty seconds, and consists of eight required

Sarah Hughes of the Skating Club of New York finishes her short program with a spin at the 2000 U.S. Figure Skating Championships in Cleveland, Ohio.

elements (jumps, spins, and footwork) that each skater must perform to the music of her choice. A missed or failed element results in a mandatory deduction. For example, a skater who omits a jump in the program loses 0.5 from her score. Because each skater must perform the same elements, the judges are able to compare the skaters and their abilities to execute the specified moves. The short program accounts for one-third of the skater's total score.

The junior or senior free skate for girls and women lasts for four minutes (the men's program lasts four minutes and thirty seconds) and counts for two-thirds of the final score. Unlike the short program, there are no specific required elements. Instead, the skater, along with her coach and choreographer, selects the elements that show her technical and presentational abilities to their best advantage. A skater puts her finest and most interesting moves in the free program. For example, you will often see Michelle Kwan's unique change-of-edge spiral or her Charlotte spiral in her long program because they show her extraordinary flexibility and stability. When Tara Lipinski was competing in the eligible ranks, she was the first woman to land the difficult triple loop-triple loop combination, so she put it in her Olympic program to show the judges her technical ability. This is also where most of the jumping occurs. Today in competitive free programs, senior ladies are landing as many as seven triple jumps, including triple-triple combinations.

The judges consider many things, including the difficulty, quality, and intricacy of the moves; the speed of the skating; how

Fun Facts and Figures

O Number of required elements in the short program: **8**

O Number of women who have landed a triple axel in competition: **2 (Midori Ito and Tonya Harding)**

O Number of revolutions in a triple axel: **3.5**

O Youngest U.S. and world champion: **(Tara Lipinski, fourteen years old, in 1997)**

O Most perfect 6.0s earned at the U.S. championships: **16 (Michelle Kwan)**

O Cost for custom skating boots, excluding blades: **about $600**

O Annual cost to finance an elite skating career: **$32,000 to $60,000**

O Age a skater must be to participate in the world championships: **fifteen by July 1 of the previous year**

O Most U.S. national championships: **9 (Maribel Vinson)**

O Most world championships: **10 (Sonja Henie)**

O Number of U.S. titles Michelle Kwan has: **5 (1996, 1998, 1999, 2000, 2001)**

O Most world medals by a U.S. skater: **6 (Carol Heiss, 5 gold, 1 silver)**

O Number of members in the U.S. Figure Skating Association: **65,299**

O Number of members in Skate Canada: **191,000**

Athlete Profile: Michelle Kwan

Michelle Kwan, 1998 Olympic silver medalist, was born in Torrence, California, on July 7, 1980. She began skating when she was five years old after watching her older brother playing hockey. At age twelve, Michelle, eager to get to the nationals and the Olympics, secretly took and passed her senior test, even though her coach had advised her to stay in the junior level for another year. Later that year, after winning the Pacific Coast sectionals, Michelle competed at nationals, placing sixth. In 1993, Kwan qualified for the Olympic team as an alternate.

Over the next seven years, Michelle became the most successful skater of her generation. She has been on the podium, usually in first place, at nearly every competition that she has entered. It is not just her success and her unparalleled style on the ice, however, that sets her apart. She strives to find a balance in her life: "It has been hard balancing school and skating, but I don't think either can wait." Her positive mental attitude helped her handle the disappointment of not winning the Olympic gold medal. Her philosophy on reaching her goals? "I know I can do it."

Athlete Profile: Taylor Webster

Taylor Webster began skating when she was eight, after she attended a friend's skating birthday party. After just a few

Michelle Kwan has scored sixteen perfect 6.0s at U.S. championships, more than any other skater.

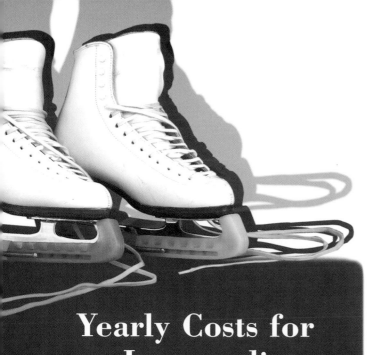

Yearly Costs for an Intermediate-Level Competitive Figure Skater

Coaching	$20,000
Ice time	$ 6,000
Costumes and clothing	$ 1,500
Boots	$ 1,200
Blades (one set every nine months)	$ 800
Competition entry fees	$ 1,000
Travel	$ 2,000
Total per year	**$32,500**

years, she and her parents moved from Florida to live near a world-class training facility. By the age of twelve, she was training at the intermediate level and dreaming of going to the Olympics.

Taylor's day begins at 5:00 AM. After stretching and warming up, she is on the ice by 6:40 AM at the University of Delaware for the first of six on-ice sessions each day. At 8:30 AM, she leaves for school and returns to the rink at 3:00 PM for off-ice conditioning (including weight training and dance classes) before skating three more sessions. She finishes skating at 8:00 PM, then goes home for dinner and to do homework.

Taylor exhibits natural grace as she bends into a beautifully positioned and perfectly centered layback spin and smiles often when she talks about skating. She's realistic about her dreams and says, "I want to get through all my tests, even if I don't compete. My long-term goal is to get to the Olympics, but my goal this year is to get to the junior nationals and do the best I can there."

Skating on a high level at a top training facility can be prohibitively costly. Many parents take second jobs, mortgage their homes, and make cross-country moves to better support their child's skating ambitions. However, skating at a city recreational facility or a mall rink, many of which have good ice surfaces and qualified coaches, can be a lot cheaper—and a lot of fun.

Taylor Webster and her family have made big sacrifices to help her pursue figure skating.

4 A Future in Figure Skating

If you choose to skate competitively, there's a good chance that you'll be able to enjoy the sport for many years to come. Although most Olympic-eligible competitive careers end when a skater has reached her mid-twenties, there are some notable exceptions. Maria Butyrskaya of Russia, 1999 world champion, was twenty-six years old when she won her world gold medal. She is still competing in the eligible ranks and plans to compete, when she will be twenty-nine, in the 2002 Olympic Games in Salt Lake City, Utah. Professional skaters can continue their careers for much longer.

Realistically, very few skaters ever make it to championship-level skating and to the Olympic Games. A maximum of three female skaters from each country is allowed to compete in the

Many professional figure skaters, such as Surya Bonaly, tour the world performing in ice shows.

Olympics, and only one gold medal is awarded every four years. Obviously, the chances of becoming an Olympic gold medalist are very slim. If you are investing in skating only to win a gold medal, you may be disappointed. Ask yourself why you want to skate. What do you hope to achieve? How much time and money are you able to devote to it?

Though the odds are against winning an individual Olympic or world medal, there are several other ways to go in competitive or professional skating. You may want to try pairs skating, ice dancing, or synchronized skating. Many skaters get jobs in touring ice shows like the Ice Capades or Disney on Ice. Others find that their talents lie in teaching and work as coaches or choreographers. Some former skaters even work as sports journalists. Then again, many girls and women skate recreationally all of their lives, are happy with the sport as they perform it, and are satisfied never to compete.

Above all, whatever you decide to do in skating, do it because you enjoy it. Michelle Kwan says, "I'm happy where I am. I love what I'm doing." Taylor Webster's reason for skating is, "Not so much to be a professional or to be famous, but because I love it."

So, if you are ready to skate, there is no better time to get started. Good luck!

Pursuing figure skating requires hard work and dedication—just ask these young skaters at a United States Figure Skating Association event.

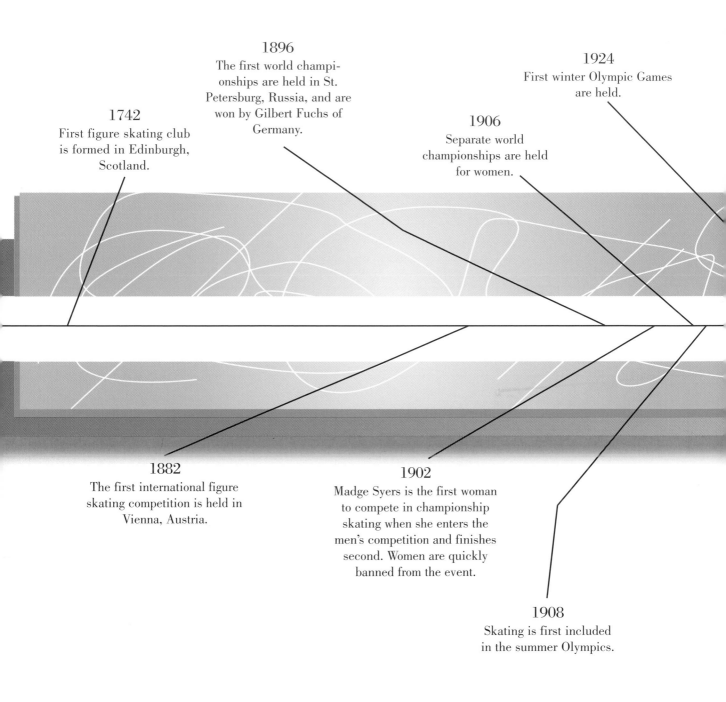

1896
The first world championships are held in St. Petersburg, Russia, and are won by Gilbert Fuchs of Germany.

1924
First winter Olympic Games are held.

1742
First figure skating club is formed in Edinburgh, Scotland.

1906
Separate world championships are held for women.

1882
The first international figure skating competition is held in Vienna, Austria.

1902
Madge Syers is the first woman to compete in championship skating when she enters the men's competition and finishes second. Women are quickly banned from the event.

1908
Skating is first included in the summer Olympics.

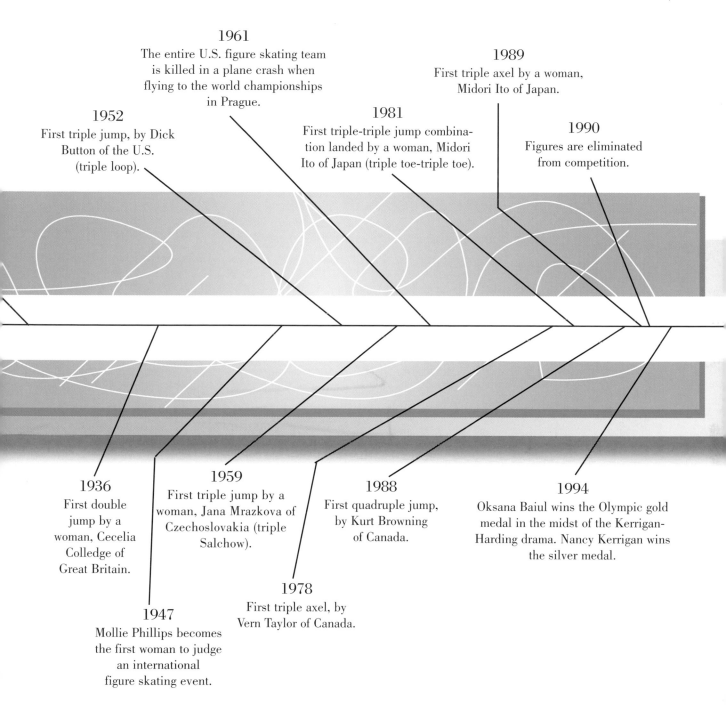

1961
The entire U.S. figure skating team is killed in a plane crash when flying to the world championships in Prague.

1989
First triple axel by a woman, Midori Ito of Japan.

1952
First triple jump, by Dick Button of the U.S. (triple loop).

1981
First triple-triple jump combination landed by a woman, Midori Ito of Japan (triple toe-triple toe).

1990
Figures are eliminated from competition.

1936
First double jump by a woman, Cecelia Colledge of Great Britain.

1959
First triple jump by a woman, Jana Mrazkova of Czechoslovakia (triple Salchow).

1988
First quadruple jump, by Kurt Browning of Canada.

1994
Oksana Baiul wins the Olympic gold medal in the midst of the Kerrigan-Harding drama. Nancy Kerrigan wins the silver medal.

1947
Mollie Phillips becomes the first woman to judge an international figure skating event.

1978
First triple axel, by Vern Taylor of Canada.

Glossary

edge   Each skate has an inside and an outside edge with a hollow in the middle. A skater can skate on an inside or an outside edge, going either forward or backward.

edge jump   A jump that takes off from an edge without using the other foot to assist. The axel, Salchow, and loop are edge jumps.

free leg   The leg that is not on the ice.

free skate   A four-minute program that counts for two-thirds of a skater's score in girls' or women's competitions.

rotation   The direction of a turn, jump, or spin. This can be clockwise or counterclockwise. Most skaters have a decided preference for one direction over the other.

short program   A two-minute-and-forty-second program made up of eight required elements. Failure to complete an element results in a mandatory deduction. The short program counts for one-third of a skater's score in competition.

spiral   An arabesque move in which the skater extends her free foot in the air behind her. A spiral can be executed moving forward or backward, on an inside edge or an outside edge, in a straight line or on a curve. The move shows flexibility.

stroking   A movement in which the skater pushes off from the inside edge of each skating foot alternately to gain speed.

three-turn   A turn, done on one skate, that involves changing both edge and direction. For example, a forward right three-turn begins on the right inside edge, going forward, and finishes on the right outside edge, going backward. The tracing on the ice looks like the number three.

toe jump   A jump that takes off assisted by a toe pick.

toe pick   The teeth on the front of a figure skating blade.

e-mail: skatecanada@skatecanada.ca
Web site: http://www.cfsa.ca

Web Sites

Figure Skater's Website
www.sk8stuff.com

Recreational Figure Skating FAQ
www.cyberus.ca/~karen/recskate

Skater's Edge
www.skatersedgemag.com

SkateWeb
www.frogsonice.com/skateweb

Slam!
www.canoe.ca/SLAM/home.html

Technical Figure Skating
www.northstarnet.org/eakhome/skating/kevinnew

For Further Reading

Boitano, Brian (with Suzanne Harper). *Boitano's Edge: Inside the Real World of Figure Skating*. New York: Simon and Schuster, 1997.

Boo, Michael. *The Story of Figure Skating*. New York: William Morrow, 1998.

Kwan, Michelle. *The Winning Attitude! What It Takes to Be a Champion*. New York: Hyperion, 1999.

Milton, Steve. *Skate: 100 Years of Figure Skating*. North Pomfret, VT: Trafalgar Square, 1996.

Milton, Steve. *Super Skaters*. Avenel, NJ: Crescent Books, 1997.

Morrissey, Peter, and James Young. *Figure Skating School*. Ontario, Canada: Firefly, 1996.

About the Author

Kathryn M. Moncrief is an assistant professor of English at Washington College in Chestertown, Maryland. She is also a recreational figure skater and skating writer for the online magazine *Sportsjones*.

Photo Credits

Cover photos by Maura Boruchow; pp. 3, 11, 36, 47, 49, 51, 54, 56, 59, 61 © Kathryn M. Moncrief; pp. 5, 12, 16, 18, 19, 20, 21, 23, 24, 25, 26, 27, 28, 30, 32, 33, 46, 48 by Maura Boruchow; p. 6 © Everett Collection; p. 9, 15, 17, 45 © Corbis; p. 34 © Agence Vandystadt/Allsport; p. 37 © Richard Martin/Agence Vandystadt/Allsport; p. 39 © Brian Bahr/Allsport; pp. 57, 63 © Frank J. Zamboni & Co., Inc. Diagrams on pp. 4, 52–53 by Tom Forget.

Thanks to The Skating Club of Hingham at Pilgrim Arena, Hingham, MA.

Series Design

Danielle Goldblatt

Layout

Claudia Carlson